Repeat The Sounding Joy

Daily Advent Devotional For Teens

MICHAEL ARMSTRONG HALL

Foreword

Don't let advent rush by this year.

Slow down and be filled with the joy of Christmas as you turn your attention towards Jesus.

In the midst of the busyness of December, take 5 minutes and allow these daily devotional readings to guide you into the awe and wonder of the incarnation. Bible insights and questions for reflection will help you make sense of the Christmas story and its relevance to everyday life.

Table of Contents

1 – Light vs Darkness

> *The people who walked in darkness have seen a great light; those who dwelt in a land of deep darkness, on them has light shone.*

Isaiah 9:2

Darkness is the absence of light. You can not fill a room with *darkness* - you make the room dark by removing the light. Darkness is no match for light. The presence of light drives darkness away. The arrival of Jesus into the world is described as a great light for people walking in darkness.

Imagine living in a permanently dark room. We might learn where things are by touch and be able to do some simple tasks, but it wouldn't be anything like life in the light. Things go wrong in the dark. In a dark world we are stumbling around, making mistakes, hurting ourselves and others. Walking in darkness leads to problems. But when a great light arrives, suddenly walking becomes a lot easier.

The arrival of Jesus into the world is described as the dawn of light for those living in a land of deep darkness. We are surrounded by darkness in a broken world. The birth of Jesus is a shaft of light breaking through, giving us hope.

When viewed in the light of Jesus, life makes sense. We see our mistakes clearly and are empowered to live more like him. We see others more clearly and are inspired to love and serve them. We see the gifts God has given us more clearly and are set free to glorify God by enjoying them with gratitude. That is the good news of the Christmas message!

- What areas of your life feel most dark?
- Where can you see the light of Jesus breaking through in your life and the lives of those around you?

2 – A Gift

> *For to us a child is born, to us a son is given*
>
> Isaiah 9:6

Jesus is a child born **to us**. He is **given** to us as a gift. His birth in Bethlehem is not just good news for the world. It is good news for each one of us in a personal way. He knows you and He came for **you**.

Imposter syndrome is the feeling that you don't belong. It is the belief that people have an incorrect view of your capabilities or character and you could be exposed as a fraud at any time. Christians can also experience this, with a nagging doubt that God could really love *me*. You do not find yourself in God's kingdom because He loves the world and you qualify as a technicality. He loves you personally.

How do we know that love? He has demonstrated it to us in the most powerful way. In the manger. On the cross. And in the empty tomb. God enters the world in humble circumstances. He has every right to come in judgement against a rebellious people but, instead, He chose to come on a rescue mission.

He comes not to be served but to serve. He makes himself weak and helpless as a child so that we can find strength in Him. He humbly submits to death on a cross so that we can be given the gift of eternal life.

Jesus, the son, is *given* to us. We have not earned his incarnation. We don't deserve his love and salvation. He comes to us in grace and mcrcy. We have nothing to offer. We can receive Jesus with empty hands.

- Do you find yourself trying to earn acceptance and approval from other people? In what ways?
- How does God's freely-given grace affect your life?

3 – A Sign

> *Therefore the Lord himself will give you a sign. Behold, the virgin shall conceive and bear a son, and shall call his name Immanuel.*
>
> Isaiah 7:14

Have you ever wished that God would make himself more visible? Has anyone ever told you that they would believe in God if he would give them an obvious sign?

More than 500 years before the birth of Jesus, God said that he would give his people a 'sign'. That sign would be a son born to a virgin. A very unlikely sign! Those who heard this prophecy and believed it died without seeing it come to pass. Over generations, some still waited, clinging onto hope while others forgot or disbelieved. Then, something happened.

This is how the birth of Jesus the Messiah came about: His mother Mary was pledged to be married to Joseph, but before they came together, she was found to be pregnant through the Holy Spirit.

Matthew 1:18

All this took place to fulfill what the Lord had said through the prophet: "The virgin will conceive and give birth to a son, and they will call him Immanuel" (which means "God with us").

Matthew 1:22-23

The words spoken by Isaiah are fulfilled in Mary's conception. This is the moment God had foretold. A virgin had conceived through the power of the Holy Spirit. This miraculous event is God entering into humanity. This is much more than God sending an angel. It is different to God's presence descending as a pillar of fire in the wilderness or a cloud in the tabernacle. He has not just appeared out of thin air. He is *born.*

The miraculous conception shows us Jesus' divinity - this is no ordinary boy. But his gestation and birth show us Jesus' humanity - this is God become man. The sign that God is with his people is that he has become like us.

> *"The Virgin Birth alone insured both the full deity and full humanity of Jesus. If God had created Jesus a complete human being in heaven and sent Him to earth apart from any human parent, it is difficult to see how He could be truly a man. If God had sent His Son into the world through both a human father and mother, it is difficult to see how He could be truly God."*
>
> Sam Storms

Isaiah told God's people to look for a sign - a virgin birth. A sign is only useful because it points to something. The virgin birth is a great sign, but don't stop at the sign. Look towards the person the sign is pointing to. The virgin birth did not occur just so we could marvel at the miracle but so we could look at the one who was born. A Son. Jesus.

- When you think of Jesus, are you more likely to think about his divinity (Jesus is God) or his humanity (Jesus is human)?
- How can your life be a sign that points towards Jesus?

4 – Names

> *For to us a child is born, to us a son is given; and the government shall be upon his shoulder, and his name shall   be   called Wonderful Counselor, Mighty   God, Everlasting Father, Prince of Peace.*

Isaiah 9:6

The child born at Christmas is the King of Kings who will rule the universe for eternity!

The **government will be upon his shoulders**, which takes the weight off yours. If you are feeling weighed down and burdened, this is great news. The good news of Christmas is that we do not have to bear the weight of the world on our shoulders, Jesus invites us to rest in him.

Jesus is the **Wonderful Counsellor**. He knows you more deeply than anyone else does. This is not cold, detached information

– He loves you and guides you in wisdom. There is no better counsellor. The good news of Christmas is that we are known and loved by Jesus who will graciously give us all the wisdom we need.

Jesus is the **Mighty God**. There is no situation that is beyond his power. He spoke the universe into existence and He holds it together. There is nothing that He can't do for us. The good news of Christmas is that the mighty God is declaring his love for us.

Jesus is the **Everlasting Father**. It can be confusing that Jesus, the Son, is referred to as 'Father' in Isaiah's prophesy. Father is best understood here as *'source'*. Jesus is the source of our life, everything exists by him, through him and for him.

Jesus is the **Prince of Peace**. We live in a world where peace is hard to find. Our peace can come and go quickly based on circumstances which are often beyond our control. But Jesus arrives with a message of peace on earth. He is the prince of peace that can bring rest to our hearts, no matter the situation surrounding us.

- Which of the names of Jesus mentioned in these verses stands out most to you?
- How are these attributes displayed in your family?

5 – Waiting

Then an angel of the Lord appeared to him, standing at the right side of the altar of incense. When Zechariah saw him, he was startled and was gripped with fear. But the angel said to him: "Do not be afraid, Zechariah; your prayer has been heard. Your wife Elizabeth will bear you a son, and you are to call him John. He will be a joy and delight to you, and many will rejoice because of his birth, for he will be great in the sight of the Lord. He is never to take wine or other fermented drink, and he will be filled with the Holy Spirit even before he is born. He will bring back many of the people of Israel to the Lord their God. And he will go on before the Lord, in the spirit and power of Elijah, to turn the hearts of the parents to their children and the disobedient to the wisdom of the righteous—to make ready a people prepared for the Lord."

Luke 1:11-17

The birth of John the Baptist is the fulfilment of prophecies made by Malachi's 400 years earlier[1]. God's people have been waiting a long time for those words to be fulfilled.

The fulfilment of the long-awaited messenger takes place by answering another, more personal, wait. Zechariah and Elizabeth had desperately wanted a child but were unable to conceive. The angel who delivers this message to Zechariah declares

[1] *"I will send my messenger, who will prepare the way before me. Then suddenly the Lord you are seeking will come to his temple; the messenger of the covenant, whom you desire, will come," says the Lord Almighty.*

Malachi 3:1

"See, I will send the prophet Elijah to you before that great and dreadful day of the Lord comes. He will turn the hearts of the parents to their children, and the hearts of the children to their parents; or else I will come and strike the land with total destruction."

Malachi 4:5-6

the fulfilment of Malachi's prophecy, but he doesn't start there. He starts by announcing that Zechariah's prayer has been heard - they would have a son who will bring them joy and delight.

God could have fulfilled Malachi's prophecy in many different ways, but he chose to fulfil it through the birth of a boy to a couple who longed for a child. God's plans and purposes bring joy to everyone involved. God's brings about his eternal purposes by blessing his people.

As we wait we can have confidence that God never stops working and his purposes involve great joy and delight for us.

- What is the most difficult waiting experience you have had?
- What difference does God make to your waiting?

6 – He Will Save

> *She will bear a son, and you shall call his name Jesus, for he will save his people from their sins."*

Matthew 1:21

Why did the angel specify his name? Jesus could have done everything He did with a different name. The name Jesus is unique to us but was not unusual at the time, so what was the point of this name?

This was a name with meaning. It means to rescuer or saviour. This is what Jesus came to do. He was a powerful and wise teacher but his primary purpose was not to tell us what to do. He did many wonderful miracles but his primary mission was not to heal every sick person on the Earth. His primary purpose was to save us.

We can sometimes think of Christmas as a bit of a boost, a pep talk to remind us to be nicer to each other, but Jesus has come to do something much better than that.

Imagine yourself in a pit that you can't get out of. It's no use having someone come along and tell you what you should have done to avoid falling in. It's no use having someone tell you how they would get out - because you're stuck. The good news of Christmas is that Jesus climbs down into the pit to lift you out!

Jesus offers something better than whatever we think we need. The Jews at the time of Jesus wanted a king to conquer the Romans and make their lives a bit easier - Jesus offers an entirely new life. He did not bring a better political or military solution. His mission was far bigger – IIe is the ultimatc, eternal king who is charge of the universe!

He knows us better than we know ourselves and he offers a life of joy that transcends culture, country and circumstances.

- What sin do you need to confess and receive forgiveness for?

- What experiences have you had of Jesus rescuing you from your own bad decisions?

7 – Insignificant

> *Now the birth of Jesus Christ took place in this way. When his mother Mary had been betrothed to Joseph, before they came together she was found to be with child from the Holy Spirit. And her husband Joseph, being a just man and unwilling to put her to shame, resolved to divorce her quietly. But as he considered these things, behold, an angel of the Lord appeared to him in a dream, saying, "Joseph, son of David, do not fear to take Mary as your wife, for that which is conceived in her is from the Holy Spirit.*

> Matthew 1:18-20

What does it mean to be significant? We can often feel insignificant. You may feel like no one really cares about you. Even if you do have loving family and friends, they represent a tiny fraction of the human beings on this planet. Our lives are a tiny proportion of time within human history.

When we think about the big picture, we are insignificant in many ways.

While most of the world does not know your name, does not know anything about you and does not really care what is going on in your life, God does! No one is insignificant before God.

God enters human history through a young woman and her fiancée. They were not significant people in the world's eyes. God's plan that has been building up for thousands of years is coming to fruition but there is no big launch, bright lights or marketing campaign. It doesn't seem like the way you or I would do it!

We know very little about Joseph other than his ancestry and his willingness to listen to God in a complicated situation. We think of significance as power, fame or popularity. God thinks of significance as an unknown man who will listen to his word and trust what he says.

"Significance is about who we are before it is about what we do."

John Ortberg

- What makes you feel significant?
- How do you need submit to God's word today?

8 – God With Us

> *Behold, the virgin shall conceive and bear a son, and they shall call his name Immanuel (which means, God with us)*

> Matthew 1:23

God's plan has always been to dwell with his people. This starts in the garden of Eden where God walked with Adam in the cool of the day.

When sin enters the world, this relationship is broken but, despite mankind's repeated rebellion, God continues to move towards us in love.

Through the tabernacle and temple systems we see God's presence dwelling in the midst of his people.

"Then have them make a sanctuary for me, and I will dwell among them. Make this tabernacle and all its furnishings exactly like the pattern I will show you"

Exodus 25:8-9

This is a big deal. God doesn't have to live amongst his rebellious people. God's presence dwelling in the tabernacle shows the love of God and his desire to gather a people to himself. It is great news that God wants to dwell in the midst of his people, but his people (then and now) are sinful and he is not. He is holy and they (and we) are not.

A complex sacrificial system was needed because sin naturally brings separation from a holy God.

The birth of Jesus represents something different. Isaiah said that Jesus would be known as "Immanuel". Matthew recounts this prophecy and explains what that word means - "God with us". God the Son came to live among us to deal with our sin that separates us from Him. He has demonstrated His love for us – He is with us.

> *"If we could condense all the truths of Christmas into only three words, these would be the words: 'God with us.'"*

John MacArthur

- What happens when you forget God is with you?
- What difference does God's presence make to your sense of identity?

9 – He Shall Be Called

In the sixth month the angel Gabriel was sent from God to a city of Galilee named Nazareth, to a virgin betrothed to a man whose name was Joseph, of the house of David. And the virgin's name was Mary. And he came to her and said, "Greetings, O favored one, the Lord is with you!" But she was greatly troubled at the saying, and tried to discern what sort of greeting this might be. And the angel said to her, "Do not be afraid, Mary, for you have found favor with God. And behold, you will conceive in your womb and bear a son, and you shall call his name Jesus. He will be great and will be called the Son of the Most High. And the Lord God will give to him the throne of his father David, and he will reign over the house of Jacob forever, and of his kingdom there will be no end."

And Mary said to the angel, "How will this be, since I am a virgin?"

And the angel answered her, "The Holy Spirit will come upon you, and the power of the Most High will overshadow you; therefore the child to be born will be called holy—the Son of God.

Luke 1:26-35

The angel Gabriel says 55 words (in the English translation) to Mary and 46 of those are about his name and what he will do. Mary probably stopped listening after the first sentence revealed she would conceive, but Gabriel's announcement has a focus on who this baby is and what he will do.

The language used makes it clear that this child is a King. He will be given a throne. But not just any throne – the throne of his ancestor David. He is a descendant of the greatest king in Israel's history.

However, Jesus is not just another king like David. Mary is told that He will reign forever! There will be no end to His kingdom. There will never be a time when

Jesus is overthrown or ceases to be on the throne of the Universe. He is the King of Kings. He is in charge and will rule for eternity.

When we hear the word 'king' at Christmas, we are likely to start humming 'We Three Kings of Orient Are'. Don't lose sight of the true King of Christmas. The King of History. The King of Eternity. King Jesus.

- How does Jesus' authority as King challenge your own view of independence?
- How does your relationship with your parents help you understand Jesus' authority as King?

10 – The Servant of the Lord

And Mary said to the angel, "How will this be, since I am a virgin?" And the angel answered her, "The Holy Spirit will come upon you, and the power of the Most High will overshadow you; therefore the child to be born will be called holy—the Son of God. And behold, your relative Elizabeth in her old age has also conceived a son, and this is the sixth month with her who was called barren. For nothing will be impossible with God." And Mary said, "Behold, I am the servant of the Lord; let it be to me according to your word." And the angel departed from her.

Luke 1:34-38

The anticipation of celebrating Christmas often eclipses the reality. We can enjoy the celebrations, but things rarely go exactly as planned. On a bigger scale, has your life turned out as expected?! Nobody knows how their life will turn out. Our lives twist and turn as the result of incidents and interactions which we have no control over.

In an uncertain world, we can find assurance knowing that, while our future is unclear to us, it is known and directed by a God who loves us.

To say Mary's life took an unexpected turn would be the biggest understatement in history! What is her response? To humbly submit and trust God. She hears the word of the Lord and believes it.

Life does not always make sense to us. We might find ourselves in a different place to we expected. We might think we are going backwards despite trying to do the right thing. The solution is not to try and gain more control, because that is impossible. The solution is to trust in the God who is in control, and who loves us.

- What expectations do you have for your life as an adult?

- What responsibilities are you finding difficult at the moment? Pray that you would trust God in those areas.

11 – My Soul Magnifies the Lord

And Mary said,

"My soul magnifies the Lord,

and my spirit rejoices in God my Savior,

for he has looked on the humble estate of his servant.

For behold, from now on all generations will call me blessed;

for he who is mighty has done great things for me,

and holy is his name.

And his mercy is for those who fear him

from generation to generation.

He has shown strength with his arm;

he has scattered the proud in the thoughts of their hearts;

he has brought down the mighty from their thrones

and exalted those of humble estate;

he has filled the hungry with good things,

and the rich he has sent away empty.

He has helped his servant Israel,

in remembrance of his mercy,

as he spoke to our fathers,

to Abraham and to his offspring forever."

Luke 1:46-55

After her encounter with Gabriel, Mary goes to visit her cousin Elizabeth. As they both marvel at the miraculous pregnancies, Mary responds in a song of praise that has become known as the Magnificat.

Mary praises God. While her mind is no doubt full of questions and concerns, she lifts her eyes and declares the glory of God.

Mary rejoices in God's blessings to her. She recognizes her humble position, that she does not deserve God's favour but that he has graciously blessed her anyway. The God that Mary worships is not a cold, distant force but a living, personal God who showers love on his people.

Mary declares the greatness of God's plans. She sees his work through history towards this moment. She sees his hand in opposing the oppressor and protecting the weak. She sees the fulfilment of his promises to his people, beginning with Abraham and echoing down the family tree.

This is the God we worship at Christmas. A great God who demonstrates his glory by blessing his people. A God who never fails to keep his promises.

- Which part of Mary's song stands out to you?
- Which promises of God do you need to remember today?

12 – The Empire

> *In those days a decree went out from Caesar Augustus that all the world should be registered. This was the first registration when Quirinius was governor of Syria. And all went to be registered, each to his own town. And Joseph also went up from Galilee, from the town of Nazareth, to Judea, to the city of David, which is called Bethlehem, because he was of the house and lineage of David, to be registered with Mary, his betrothed, who was with child.*

Luke 2:1-5

The prophet Micah had prophesied that the Messiah would be born in the town of Bethlehem[2]. This could have happened in

---

[2] *"But you, Bethlehem Ephrathah, though you are small among the clans of Judah, out of you will come for me one who will be ruler over Israel, whose origins are from of old from*

any way God chose. God could have chosen to use a couple of people who already lived in Bethlehem. God could have orchestrated the events of Mary's life so that she was already living in Bethlehem.

However, that is not the way that God did it. He used a census called by a pagan emperor to bring about the birth of His Son in Bethlehem. Caesar Augustus did not know he was doing God's work when he decided to call the census. Quirinius did not give a second thought to God as he organized this census. The thousands of people travelling back to their hometown to be registered did not recognize the hand of God in these events. But, even when we can't see it, God is working. God was going to bless his people. The Messiah would be born in Bethlehem.

Have you ever felt, like me, little and insignificant in a world of seven billion people, where all the news is of big political and economic and ~~social movements and of~~ ancient times."* Micah 5:2

outstanding people with lots of power and prestige? If you have, don't let that make you disheartened or unhappy. For it is implicit in Scripture that all the mammoth political forces and all the giant industrial complexes, without their even knowing it, are being guided by God, not for their own sake but for the sake of God's little people— the little Mary and the little Joseph who have to be got from Nazareth to Bethlehem. God wields an empire to bless his children[3].

John Piper

- How have you seen God's plan at work in your life so far?
- How do God's unstoppable plans affect your confidence?

---

[3] John Piper, Good News of Great Joy

13 – Small

> *But you, O Bethlehem Ephrathah,*
> *who are too little to be among the*
> *clans of Judah, from you shall come*
> *forth for me one who is to be ruler*
> *in Israel, whose coming forth is*
> *from of old, from ancient days.*
>
> Micah 5:2

Micah's prophecy specifically describes Bethlehem as small. It was such an insignificant town that it could barely be counted among the clans of Judah. Jesus did not arrive in impressive surroundings.

But Micah's prophesy about Bethlehem also describes the significance of the one who was going to be born there. Jesus will be the ruler of Israel, originating from ancient times. The eternal living word, the king of kings, was born in a small, insignificant town. Out of something small came something very big!

"The hinge of history is on the door of a Bethlehem stable."

Ralph Washington Sockman

His parents were nobodies. His birthplace was nowhere. But his birth was so momentous that it is celebrated around the world two thousand years later!

- Where have you seen God use small things in your life to do something big?
- How can you avoid the error of overlooking things that appear small and insignificant?

14 – Weak and Helpless

And while they were there, the time came for her to give birth. And she gave birth to her firstborn son and wrapped him in swaddling cloths and laid him in a manger, because there was no place for them in the inn.

Luke 2:6-7

God enters the world in humble circumstances. He has every right to come in judgement against a rebellious people but, instead, he chooses to come on a rescue mission.

"The Almighty appeared on earth as a helpless human baby, needing to be fed and changed and taught to talk like any other child. The more you think about it, the more staggering it gets. Nothing in fiction is so fantastic as this truth of the Incarnation."

J. I. Packer

Jesus becoming a baby is crazy. At one time he was unable to support himself, living in Mary's womb. At one time the same hand that flung stars into space was unable to be lifted or grip properly. At one time the living word of God, who was there as creation was spoken into existence, was unable to speak words.

Jesus was willing to humble himself, arriving in the world weak and helpless – for us. When we comprehend that, we can be sure that there is nothing else he will withhold from us. He is willing to give everything for us. He humbly submits to death on a cross so that we can be given the gift of eternal life.

Man's maker was made man,

that He, Ruler of the stars, might nurse at His mother's breast;

that the Bread might hunger,

the Fountain thirst,

the Light sleep,

the Way be tired on its journey;

that the Truth might be accused of false witness,

the Teacher be beaten with whips,

the Foundation be suspended on wood;

that Strength might grow weak;

that the Healer might be wounded;

that Life might die.

Augustine of Hippo

- In what ways do you feel weak?
- How does Jesus challenge your understanding of strength and weakness?

15 – Good News

And in the same region there were shepherds out in the field, keeping watch over their flock by night. And an angel of the Lord appeared to them, and the glory of the Lord shone around them, and they were filled with great fear. 10 And the angel said to them, "Fear not, for behold, I bring you good news of great joy that will be for all the people. For unto you is born this day in the city of David a Savior, who is Christ the Lord.

Luke 2:8-11

God sends an angel to announce the birth of His Son to some shepherds in a field outside Jerusalem. The birth of Jesus is described as **good news** of great joy for all people.

The message of Christmas is good news not advice.

We think that Christmas offers advice about how to live life better - celebrate, spend time with family and friends, give gifts. This is all good advice, but the message of Christmas is described as good **news**. Good advice would be to start saving some money each month to prepare for the expense of Christmas next year. Good news would be that a sum of money has been deposited in your account. We act on advice. We receive news.

Advice tells us what to do to achieve a desired outcome. That is not what Jesus came to do. The message of who Jesus is and what He has done is often called the gospel – which literally means good news. The message of Christmas is not advice about how to be good, it is good news about an event that has happened. Jesus has arrived, this changes everything.

- Think of a friend or family member who does not know Jesus. How would the good news of Jesus affect their particular life circumstances?

- What happens if someone only sees Christianity as good advice rather than good news?

16 – Great Joy

And in the same region there were shepherds out in the field, keeping watch over their flock by night. And an angel of the Lord appeared to them, and the glory of the Lord shone around them, and they were filled with great fear. 10 And the angel said to them, "Fear not, for behold, I bring you good news of great joy that will be for all the people. For unto you is born this day in the city of David a Savior, who is Christ the Lord.

Luke 2:8-11

The angel's announcement of the birth of Jesus is good news of **great joy** for all people.

There aren't many cultural events that captivate the imagination like Christmas. We have an expectation that the holiday celebration should produce great joy - why else would we spend so long anticipating it?

But the reality is that the high of Christmas is over very quickly. Once the present have been unwrapped and the Christmas dinner has been devoured, family conflicts start to boil over. A survey in the UK pinpointed 2.59pm on the Monday after Christmas as the peak – or more accurately, trough – of the Christmas blues. It has been dubbed Moody Monday[4].

'Christmas' happiness is temporary and totally dependent on circumstances. The great joy that the angels announce exists regardless of critical relatives, financial difficulties and anti-climaxes. It is a deep lasting joy that is possible even in the most difficult circumstances. The birth of Jesus is good news that brings great joy not temporary happiness.

We often think the solution to our problems is a change of circumstances. What we actually need is a change of perspective. God can turn around any circumstances, but he

---

[4]http://www.telegraph.co.uk/news/uknews/roa d-and-rail-transport/12057271/Christmas-chaos-is-on-the-way.html

can also give joy and peace in the midst of any circumstances.

> *Weeping may stay for the night but rejoicing comes in the morning.*
>
> Psalm 30:5

- When have you experience the joy of the Lord in the middle of challenging circumstances?
- How can you help your family to experience joy today?

17 – All People

And in the same region there were shepherds out in the field, keeping watch over their flock by night. And an angel of the Lord appeared to them, and the glory of the Lord shone around them, and they were filled with great fear. 10 And the angel said to them, "Fear not, for behold, I bring you good news of great joy that will be for all the people. For unto you is born this day in the city of David a Savior, who is Christ the Lord.

Luke 2:8-11

This announcement of good news of great joy is for **all people.**

God announces the birth of His Son to an unlikely group of people. When we think of Christmas we picture cute kids in Christmas pajamas gathered around a Christmas tree. God thinks of a pregnant teenager giving birth in a place where animals live, in the

53

company of scruffy shepherds fresh from a night shift in the fields and some eastern astrologers who don't even believe in him

The cultural Christmas we celebrate is for a certain type of person - it's for 'nice' people, people with family and friends, people with the ability to buy and receive gifts. The good news of great joy that the angels announce is not just for a certain type of person. It's not just good news for rich people or westerners or religious people or people with happy families or people who've managed to convince the elf on the shelf that they've been good. It's good news of great joy for all people. Everybody. It's good news for me. It's good news for you.

This year, take time to reflect on this good news (not good advice) of great joy (not temporary happiness) for all people (not some people). The western Christmas is a nice bit of escapism from real life - the real Christmas is about Jesus entering **into** real life.

- Do you compare yourself with other people? In what ways
- How does the story of the shepherds challenge our ideas about comparison?

18 – Peace On Earth

And suddenly there was with the angel a multitude of the heavenly host praising God and saying, "Glory to God in the highest, and on earth peace among those with whom he is pleased!"

Luke 2:13-14

After an angel announces the birth of Jesus – the Saviour, the Messiah, the anointed one – to the shepherds, many more angels suddenly burst onto the scene. They can't help it! They couldn't contain themselves and started worshipping God for what was happening. The all-powerful, creator God was becoming a man to rescue us. Nothing like this had ever happened and the angels glorify God in response.

As we spend time considering the incarnation this year, may our response be like the angels – overflowing with praise and worship to our glorious God.

As we reflect on peace during advent, we think of the message of the angels. They brought a message of good news that will cause great joy for all people.

The choir of angels also burst out in song about peace on Earth. Jesus brings peace between us and God. We are rebels against God, we try and put ourselves on His throne and be king of our own lives. We deserve to be cut off by God, but the birth of Jesus announces that God is doing something much better - he is bringing peace to a rebellious people. His peace can overcome any hostility.

> *And the peace of God, which surpasses all understanding, will guard your hearts and your minds in Christ Jesus.*
>
> Philippians 4:7

- How have you experienced the peace of God in your life?

- How can you help others experience peace when they are in difficult circumstances?

19 – Glorifying God

When the angels went away from them into heaven, the shepherds said to one another, "Let us go over to Bethlehem and see this thing that has happened, which the Lord has made known to us." And they went with haste and found Mary and Joseph, and the baby lying in a manger. And when they saw it, they made known the saying that had been told them concerning this child. And all who heard it wondered at what the shepherds told them. But Mary treasured up all these things, pondering them in her heart. And the shepherds returned, glorifying and praising God for all they had heard and seen, as it had been told them.

Luke 2:15-20

After hearing the message and song of the angels, the shepherds then go and find Jesus - they didn't just think it was a nice story and then continue on as they had before. They didn't dismiss it without looking into it. They seek out the child that they had been told about.

After encountering Jesus they leave, glorifying and praising God as they go. It's a natural response to seeing who He is and what He's done. As Christians we can sometimes slip into the mindset that we *should* be thanking God, as if praise is a task for us to complete. True worship flows out of an encounter with Jesus. When we get a glimpse of his glory and grace, our hearts overflow in gratitude to Him.

The shepherds have been transformed and they let people know what they have seen and heard. These actions will have great consequences that we, and possibly the shepherds themselves, could not even imagine. Who are the people who heard about Jesus and later encountered him for themselves as a result of the shepherd's obedience?

Our lives are full of moments, big and small, that affect others. We need to live like our words and actions are important, because they are.

- What can you praise God for today?
- What difference could it make to your day today if you believe your words and actions have eternal significance?

20 – Follow the Star

> *Now after Jesus was born in Bethlehem of Judea in the days of Herod the king, behold, wise men from the east came to Jerusalem, saying, "Where is he who has been born king of the Jews? For we saw his star when it rose and have come to worship him."*

Matthew 2:1-2

The wise men, or Magi, are fascinating characters in the Christmas story. We know very little about them. They came from the East and were clearly not Jews themselves. They were astrologers studying the stars and probably worshipped other Gods.

They did not have the history and knowledge of God that the Jews had. But, while most of the Jews were oblivious to the birth of their King, the wise men had seen a sign and followed the evidence. The noticed the work of God in creation and listened to His voice.

The heavens declare the glory of God, and the sky above proclaims his handiwork. Day to day pours out speech, and night to night reveals knowledge. There is no speech, nor are there words, whose voice is not heard. Their voice goes out through all the earth, and their words to the end of the world.

Psalm 19:1-4

For what can be known about God is plain to them, because God has shown it to them. For his invisible attributes, namely, his eternal power and divine nature, have been clearly perceived, ever since the creation of the world, in the things that have been made.

Romans 1:19-20

God has not left us guessing what He is like. He has revealed himself to us. Through creation. Through His Word. And through the Living Word – Jesus. He is speaking, will we listen?

- Take some time today to look around and notice the fingerprints of God in the world around you.
- What are the barriers that prevent you listening to God's voice?

21 – The Anti-King

When Herod the king heard this, he was troubled, and all Jerusalem with him; and assembling all the chief priests and scribes of the people, he inquired of them where the Christ was to be born. They told him, "In Bethlehem of Judea, for so it is written by the prophet: "'And you, O Bethlehem, in the land of Judah, are by no means least among the rulers of Judah; for from you shall come a ruler who will shepherd my people Israel.'" Then Herod summoned the wise men secretly and ascertained from them what time the star had appeared. And he sent them to Bethlehem, saying, "Go and search diligently for the child, and when you have found him, bring me word, that I too may come and worship him."

Matthew 2:3-8

And being warned in a dream not to return to Herod, they departed to their own country by another way.

Matthew 2:12

Then Herod, when he saw that he had been tricked by the wise men, became furious, and he sent and killed all the male children in Bethlehem and in all that region who were two years old or under, according to the time that he had ascertained from the wise men.

Matthew 2:16

Herod was threatened by the birth of a so-called king and asked the Magi to tell him where they found the child, secretly planning to find and kill Jesus. They do not comply and Herod's horrific response is to slaughter every boy under two years old in Bethlehem, intending to kill Jesus among them.

Many families suffered the loss of children due to Herod's actions. Their suffering is the result of someone else's sin. God's people are being sinned against by Herod, the power-crazed king.

God's people and God's kingdom will always face opposition. the storyline of the Bible, history and our own experiences confirm this. Jesus told his followers to expect it.

We should not be surprised when we encounter pain and suffering. It is part of life in a fallen world. Suffering will exist until Jesus returns.

> *Dear friends, do not be surprised at the fiery ordeal that has come on you to test you, as though something strange were happening to you. But rejoice inasmuch as you participate in the sufferings of Christ, so that you may be overjoyed when his glory is revealed.*
>
> 1 Peter 4:12-13

This means we don't have to ignore suffering but we can engage those who are suffering with the hope of the Christmas story - that Jesus was born into a world of suffering, that he suffered on our behalf, and that we eagerly await his return when he will put an end to all suffering.

Herod the king inflicts suffering to maintain his power. Jesus the King of Kings lays down His power to suffer for us.

- How do you respond to suffering?
- How can you comfort other people who are suffering?

22 – God's Plan

Now when they had departed, behold, an angel of the Lord appeared to Joseph in a dream and said, "Rise, take the child and his mother, and flee to Egypt, and remain there until I tell you, for Herod is about to search for the child, to destroy him." And he rose and took the child and his mother by night and departed to Egypt and remained there until the death of Herod. This was to fulfil what the Lord had spoken by the prophet, "Out of Egypt I called my son."

Matthew 2:13-15

Herod's plan seemed foolproof - kill every boy and then you are bound to kill Jesus. However, God's plans are never thwarted!

Joseph is warned in a dream to go to Egypt where Jesus escapes the slaughter of the innocents.

Jesus' journey to Egypt and subsequent return, is another fulfilment of Old Testament prophecy, this time from Hosea 11:1[5]. Herod tried to use brute force to oppose God's plan. God had spoken hundreds of years earlier that this would happen, and that Herod would not prevail.

No matter what opposition, suffering and pain we experience, nothing can stop God's plans and purposes!

> *Who shall separate us from the love of Christ? Shall trouble or hardship or persecution or famine or nakedness or danger or sword? As it is written: "For your sake we face death all day long; we are considered as sheep to be slaughtered." No, in all these things we are more than conquerors through him who loved us.*
>
> Romans 8:35-37

This pattern is repeated throughout Jesus' life. He faces many threats and much

[5] When Israel was a child, I loved him, and out of Egypt I called my son – Hosea 11:1

opposition, but everything seems to work out. Then Jesus is killed - was God's plan thwarted? No! Jesus only died because it was part of his plan. The cross and the resurrection were the coronation of Jesus as the true, eternal king who had conquered Satan, sin and death.

We are now waiting for Christ's second advent. Waiting for Jesus to take his rightful place as king. Many people, powers and forces are working against that, desperate for it not to happen. But God's plan can not be thwarted, and we will live in eternity with Jesus.

- What does it mean to say that God has a plan for your life?
- When have you seen evidence of God's plan at work in your life?

23 – Bow Down

*And behold, the star that they had
seen when it rose went before them
until it came to rest over the place
where the child was. When they saw
the star, they rejoiced exceedingly
with great joy. And going into the
house, they saw the child with Mary
his mother, and they fell down and
worshiped him. Then, opening their
treasures, they offered him gifts,
gold and frankincense and myrrh.*

Matthew 2:9-11

The wise men reach the end of their long
journey and meet Jesus. An encounter with
Jesus changes people. It changed the
shepherds and the Magi respond the same
way.

They rejoice with great joy. These men are
noted for their great wisdom but the thing
that causes them great joy is Jesus. Wisdom
is a gift from God and should lead us

towards adoration of Jesus, just as it did for the Magi.

The wise men bow down and worship Jesus. In a culture where children did not have a high status, the sight of foreign noblemen bowing down to a child would have been shocking. But these men recognized who they were and who Jesus was. They humbly bowed the knee before the child who spoke the Universe into existence.

The wise men give gifts. Gold suitable for a king. Frankincense symbolising his anointing. Myrrh prophesying his death. Jesus did not need these gifts. He doesn't need anything from us. But it is part of our worship to offer the things he has given us back to him. We recognize everything we have is a gift from him and we seek to use those gifts in service of Him.

- How has meeting Jesus changed your life?
- What gifts has God given you that you can use in service of Him?

24 – The Word Became Flesh

> *And the Word became flesh and dwelt among us, and we have seen his glory, glory as of the only Son from the Father, full of grace and truth.*

> John 1:14

The first verses of the Gospel of John tell us that the Word was there in the beginning. The Word was *with* God and the Word *was* God. Now that Word has become flesh and dwelt among us.

Jesus, the divine, eternal Word became like us in order that we may become like Him.

The word used for 'dwell' in John is the word tabernacle. The tabernacle in the Old Testament was where God's presence dwelt in the midst of his people. Jesus became flesh and *tabernacled* among us! We are, through our sin and rebellion, separated from God. He is Holy and we are not. We can not exist in his presence in the same way an ice cube can not exist in a furnace. If we were to enter the presence of God, we would die. We are powerless to change that. So, God did something.

He took on flesh and dwelt among us. He clothed himself in humanity and brought his presence into our midst. Everywhere he went, his presence brought transformation. Every word He spoke and every person he touched were evidence of the light and life that flowed from Him. John says we have seen his glory, but it did not look like glory in the world's eyes. The glory of God looks like a manger, a cross and an empty tomb. God displays his glory in humility.

Through Jesus' incarnation, crucifixion and resurrection, the sin that separates us from God has been dealt with. We are welcomed into God's presence, clothed in Jesus' righteousness.

> *Let us then with confidence draw near to the throne of grace, that we*

may receive mercy and find grace to help in time of need.

Hebrews 4:16

- How do you think of yourself before God?
- How can Jesus' birth, death and resurrection fill you with confidence?

25 – Seeing God

Now there was a man in Jerusalem, whose name was Simeon, and this man was righteous and devout, waiting for the consolation of Israel, and the Holy Spirit was upon him. And it had been revealed to him by the Holy Spirit that he would not see death before he had seen the Lord's Christ. And he came in the Spirit into the temple, and when the parents brought in the child Jesus, to do for him according to the custom of the Law, he took him up in his arms and blessed God and said,

"Lord, now you are letting your servant depart in peace, according to your word; for my eyes have seen your salvation that you have prepared in the presence of all peoples, a light for revelation to the Gentiles, and for glory to your people Israel."

And there was a prophetess, Anna, the daughter of Phanuel, of the tribe of Asher. She was advanced in years, having lived with her husband seven years from when she was a virgin, and then as a widow until she was eighty-four. She did not depart from the temple, worshiping with fasting and prayer night and day. And coming up at that very hour she began to give thanks to God and to speak of him to all who were waiting for the redemption of Jerusalem.

Luke 2:25-32, 36-38

What is worship? It is not just singing, it involves everything we do in life. What is your highest priority? What do you make sacrifices of time, money and effort for? What do you think about the most? What do you worry about the most? These questions can reveal what you are worshiping.

We have seen that the Shepherds and Wise Men went away from meeting Jesus, worshipping and praising Him. The Wise

Men were seeking Jesus, following His star. The Shepherds were not seeking him, their night of work was interrupted with their encounter. But, for both groups, they left glorifying God.

Simeon and Anna encounter Jesus at the temple. They were old, faithful servants of God. They were already worshipping God with their lives but there was more to come for them. They were about to meet Jesus. Their response is an explosion of praise to God.

We can't manufacture worship – it is a natural response to seeing God. If you have ever found it hard to find the motivation to pray, read the Bible or join with God's people at church, you don't need to try harder, you need to see more of God. The more we gaze at him, the more we will be transformed into his likeliness. Come and adore Him today.

O Come let us adore Him

O come let us adore Him

O come let us adore Him

Christ the Lord

- How can you worship God today?
- What habits can you build that will help you grow in your understanding of who Jesus is and what He has done?

Made in United States
Troutdale, OR
11/09/2023

14423007R00046